Text copyright © 2003 by
The El Paso Chile Company.

Photographs copyright © 2003
by Leigh Beisch.

Library of Congress
Cataloging-in-Publication Data:

Kerr, W. Park.

Viva margarita / by W. Park Kerr ;
photographs by Leigh Beisch.

p. cm.
ISBN 0-8118-4034-4 (hardcover)
1. Margaritas.
2. Tequila. I. Title.

TX951 .K3526 2003
641.8'74--dc21

2002151472

Manufactured in China.

Designed by Michael Mabry
Prop styling by Sara Slavin
Food styling by Dan Becker
Photo assistant: Angelica Arriaga

The photographer wishes to
thank Beth at Present Past,
and Neiman Marcus for their
generous lending of props.

Distributed in Canada by
Raincoast Books
9050 Shaughnessy Street
Vancouver, British Columbia
V6P 6E5

10 9 8 7 6 5 4 3 2 1

Chronicle Books LLC
85 Second Street
San Francisco, California 94105

www.chroniclebooks.com

Dedication

To Michael Wayne McLaughlin. Dear friend, brilliant collaborator, perfectly worded co-author, food genius of our generation, and just about one of the best BBQ buddies in the world. We all miss you, especially me. Michael, this one's for you.

Acknowledgments

First, a huge thank you and hats off to Mittie Helmich for her tremendous vision, excellent taste, sense of humor, and her ability to mix up the perfect and most delicious cocktails for this book. M3, your mixology will keep us in the pink for years! The compelling photography is by San Franciscan Leigh Beisch, assisted by Angelica Arriaga. Snappy props directed by Sara Slavin, and the killer food styling by the rockin' Dan Becker. Book concept by the eminent West coast designers, Michael Mabry and Peter Soe Jr., both of Michael Mabry Design, Emeryville, California. Sarah Griffin Villarreal at El Paso Chile Company. Carolyn Coughlin's yummy culinary contributions. Special thanks to Beth at Present Past for lending us some of her treasures as props. The entire Chronicle Books team: Ben Shaykin, Amy Treadwell, Jan Hughes, Doug Ogan, Erik Sandall, and Beth Steiner. Lastly, to Bill LeBlond, an editor with style, vision, and taste. He is the the perfect model for what a cool guy looks like (and acts like) when he grows up! To all the above team, I thank you from the bottom of my heart (and glass) for all that you have done to make this tasty project all that it can be.

—W. Park Kerr

NACIONAL.

REPUBLICA

100% PURO DE AGAVE

SILVER

TEQUILA

ESTATE GROWN

40% ALC./VOL. (80 PROOF)   CONT.

table of contents

Introduction

The margarita—the drink that's a lifestyle!

It's all about a fun-loving exuberance for all things feisty, spicy, and good in life. This lively libation fuels our passion for celebrations with fire and soul, and for me, that means creating lots of great frosty and potent south-of-the-border elixirs and delicious tequila-boosted spicy-hot party dishes—all in one life-affirming ongoing fiesta!

There's a subtle seduction to Señorita Margarita that inspires an end-less quest for yet another fabulous concoction beginning with tequila and fresh-squeezed lime juice. (And besides, someone's got to do it!) Evolving from that primitive, macho, fiery "cactus water" that's slammed back with a bit of salt and lime (don't get me wrong—that libation still has a special allure all its own) is a whole new collection of Uber-ritas, ultimate margarita cocktails tweaked and gilded with lusciousness into a whole new deluxe strata. And yes, we've taken a few liberties, pushing the mixological envelope beyond the margarita; after all, all you need for a start is a bottle of tequila and some ice—and the mind reels with the possibilities.

And, never being one to limit the great magic of tequila just to the glass, I made sure it found its way into a fired-up patio party menu of spicy, savory dishes and a wondrously delicious dessert. Some are subtly kissed with a touch of tequila fire, and some go as far as to enjoy all the fragrant, citrusy attributes of a good margarita.

For a quick little Tequila 101: You can trace the margarita's roots straight to the blue agave plant. The heart of the agave is distilled into tequila and refined to produce many distinctive styles and varying degrees of quality, from the freshly distilled and fiery blanco (white) or plata (silver), and the young but smooth gold, to the "rested" and mellow reposado and the ultra-smooth aged and sippable añejo. What-ever your reference, you can always count on having the absolute best "agave experience" sipping a tequila cocktail made with 100 percent agave tequila; the premium quality is guaranteed, so look for it on the label.

The margarita's beauty and allure is steeped in mystery. In my own version of the history of the margarita, it probably was born in Jalisco, Mexico, where tequila is made, and where they have been serving up tequila with fresh lime juice and salt for eons. Around the late 1940s, when all things Latin were heating up on this side of the border, and tequila was the hot new liquor on the cocktail scene, the margarita appeared in the States.

As one story goes, a brilliant bartender substituted tequila and lime juice for the brandy and lemon juice in the classic and wildly popular sidecar—to push the new liquor—and the margarita was born.

We may never know exactly how the mixological miracle of this fiery Mexican magic came about—but one thing's for sure: The margarita is always beckoning us to celebrate the lush heat of tequila and the cit-rusy zest of orange and lime. So get out that cocktail shaker and your Mexican-lime juicer, and shake up a cold one that will put an *iay caramba!* smile on your face.

¡Salud!

south-of-the-border classics

The Ultimate Margarita, or Uber-rita

When it comes to making the ultimate margarita, the key is in the balance between the sweet, the tart, and the feisty. Sublimely simple and finely tuned, this is the perfect alchemy of 100 percent agave silver tequila, fresh lime, and Cointreau, a premium orange liqueur. Margarita traditionalists may insist on a salt rim, but the Federales won't come looking for you if your preference is for saltless margis.

1 lime wedge

Kosher salt in a small plate

1½ cups crushed ice

1½ ounces premium silver tequila

1 ounce Cointreau

1 ounce fresh lime juice

1 scant tablespoon superfine sugar

6 ice cubes

Garnish: 1 to 2 lime wedges

Run the lime wedge around the rim of a margarita glass. Dip the moistened rim in the salt. Set the lime wedge aside and chill the glass until ready to use.

Fill a cocktail shaker with the crushed ice and add the tequila, Cointreau, lime juice, and sugar. Shake vigorously to blend and chill.

Fill the prepared glass with the ice cubes. Strain the shaken mixture into the glass. Squeeze 1 or 2 lime wedges into the drink, depending on personal preference. Drop the lime wedges into the drink and serve.

tequila tip

Adding an extra citrus splash of fresh orange juice or, equally great, pineapple juice, really makes a margi come alive. Or, for real south-of-the-border flavor, use the juice of 2 small Key limes (also known as Mexican limes) in place of Persian lime juice. And, of course, you can always gild the margi with sweet Grand Marnier instead of Cointreau, for a great counterbalance to the Key limes' tartness.

Frozen Mandarina Margarita

When that sultry summer heat wave hits, the best way to cool down is to blend up a frosty pitcher of potent and fruity frozen margaritas, delivering just the right amount of arctic blast. My version includes fresh orange juice, almond-flavored amaretto, and the tangy kick of frozen lime juice cubes and citrusy mandarin sorbet. This is a fabulous way to boost the flavor factor and optimize frozen slushiness. If you can't find mandarin sorbet, orange sorbet is a perfect substitute.

4 to 8 lime wedges

1/3 cup kosher salt in a small plate

1 cup crushed ice

8 lime juice ice cubes (recipe follows)

1/2 cup mandarin sorbet

1 cup tequila

3 ounces Triple Sec

2 ounces fresh orange juice

2 ounces amaretto liqueur

Garnish: 4 lime wedges or lime wheels

Run a lime wedge or two around the rim of 4 margarita glasses. Dip the moistened rims in the salt. Chill the glasses until ready to use.

In a blender, combine all the ingredients except the lime wedges for garnish. Blend until well combined and slushy.

Pour the blended mixture evenly among the prepared glasses. Squeeze 1 lime wedge over the top of each drink and drop the wedge into the drink.

Lime Cubes

You will need about 2 cups fresh lime juice to fill an ice cube tray. Pour the mixture slowly into the ice tray until it comes up near the top. Freeze for 2 to 3 hours. Depending on the ice tray, each cube should measure out to about 1 ounce.

For a time saver, use can of frozen limeade diluted with water as a substitute; however, it will be much sweeter than fresh juice.

tequila tip	
	For a super-frosty tropical margarita, try 5 to 6 pineapple juice ice cubes in place of the mandarin sorbet, or for a cosmopolitan twist, use cranberry juice cubes. Ready-made juices and nectars are a great way to go—just look for a high content of actual juice in the ingredients. Fill the ice cube tray with the juice and freeze for 3 to 4 hours.

Smokin' Margarita

My good friend Ron Cooper makes the best damn mescal in the world. He is well known for his artisanal, small-batch mescals from small villages in the Oaxaca region of Mexico. His highly sippable, distinctly smoky Del Maguey Chichicapa mescal was the inspiration for this mescal-fueled margarita, conceived by Mark Miller of the Coyote Café.

Sipping is mandatory to enjoy all the depth and complexity of this smoldering cocktail.

1 lime wedge
Kosher salt in a small plate
6 ice cubes
1 ounce silver tequila
1 ounce lime juice
1 ounce Grand Marnier
1 ounce Mescal Chichicapa

Run the lime wedge around the rim of a 6-ounce old-fashioned glass. Dip the moistened rim in the salt. Set the lime wedge aside and chill the glass till ready to use.

Fill the prepared glass with the ice. Add the tequila, lime juice, and Grand Marnier. Stir a few revolutions until blended.

Slowly pour the mescal over the back of a spoon into the glass to float on the top of the drink and serve.

Sparkling Sunrise Cooler

Let's face it, the basic Tequila Sunrise was just begging for an upgrade, and I think this one hits the mark. Elaborating on the classic recipe, we've used Chambord in place of grenadine, added a splash of Maraska maraschino liqueur (one of Hemingway's favorites, it imparts almond overtones and is more tart than sweet), paired with the fresh kick of grapefruit juice and the traditional orange juice. Finish with a refreshing splash of chilled club soda for the cooling fizz factor, and you've got yourself a sunrise that hits a whole new level of fabulousness.

6 to 8 ice cubes
2 ounces tequila
3 ounces fresh orange juice
3 ounces fresh grapefruit juice
½ ounce maraschino liqueur
½ ounce Chambord
Splash of club soda

Garnish: 1 orange wheel,
1 mint sprig (optional)

Fill a tall 10-ounce glass with the ice. Add the tequila, orange and grapefruit juices, and maraschino liqueur. Stir to blend.

Add the Chambord, letting it swirl down. Top with club soda.

Garnish by placing the orange wheel and the mint sprig, if you like, on the rim of the glass and serve.

Nacionalista

We've taken the cool sophistication of the Cosmopolitan to fiery heights. Replacing the traditional vodka with the seductive fire of tequila, and elevating the Triple Sec with the vanilla, orange, and almond tones of Tuaca liqueur sends this cocktail to an altitude way beyond the original. In fact, once you've sipped one of these gems, you may never go back to a vodka Cosmo again.

1 lime wedge
Kosher salt in a small plate
6 ice cubes
1½ ounces tequila
1 ounce Tuaca
1 ounce cranberry juice
1 ounce fresh lime juice

Garnish: 1 lime slice,
fresh cranberries (optional)

Run the lime wedge around the rim of a 6-ounce cocktail glass. Dip the moistened rim in the salt. Set the lime wedge aside and chill the glass until ready to use.

Fill a cocktail shaker with the ice and add the tequila, Tuaca, cranberry juice, and lime juice. Shake vigorously to blend and chill.

Strain the mixture into the chilled glass. Garnish by placing the lime slice and the fresh cranberries, if you like, on the rim of the glass and serve.

Agave María

I don't know any three ingredients more perfectly suited for each other than tequila, hot sauce, and tomato juice. This spicy tequila Bloody Mary has the refreshing addition of fresh cucumber to counterbalance the hot and fiery. I prefer English, or hothouse, cucumbers (the long, skinny variety) for their great flavor and practically nonexistent seeds. We can't guarantee a visit from Mother Mary, but after a few sips, we can certainly promise an inner glow of some ethereal intensity.

Using the freshest and thickest tomato juice for this recipe will give you quality results. And for a super-spiced-up variation, try substituting pepper-infused tequila for the silver tequila to really turn up the heat. Salt the rim of your glass with a combo of kosher salt and lime zest for an extra-zesty kick.

2 ounces silver tequila

1½ ounces fresh lime juice

1 garlic clove, minced

½ cup chopped cucumber

3 to 5 dashes Worcestershire sauce

3 to 5 dashes your favorite hot sauce (to taste)

6 to 8 ice cubes

4 to 5 ounces V8 or tomato juice

Garnish: 1 lime wedge,
1 celery stalk or green onion (optional)

In a blender, combine the tequila, lime juice, garlic, cucumber, Worcestershire, and hot sauce. Blend until the cucumber is puréed and fairly smooth.

Fill a tall 8-ounce glass with ice and pour in the blended mixture. Add the V8 or tomato juice and stir until well combined.

Squeeze the lime wedge into the drink and drop the wedge into the glass. Garnish with a green onion or celery stalk, if you like, and serve.

Paloma

A classic favorite south of the border, La Paloma is traditionally made with lime juice and Squirt (the refreshingly carbonated grapefruit beverage). This version, made with lots of sweet, fresh ruby red grapefruit juice (I like to include lots of the fresh pulp), the rich warmth of añejo tequila, and a quintessential splash of Squirt, is sure to gain a following bigger than the state of Texas.

6 ice cubes

3 ounces fresh ruby red grapefruit juice

2 ounces añejo tequila

½ ounce Harlequin orange liqueur or Triple Sec

Splash of Squirt

Garnish: 1 mint sprig (optional)

In a blender, combine the ice, grapefruit juice, tequila, and orange liqueur. Blend on high speed with a few chunks of ice until frothy.

Pour the blended mixture into a tall 8-ounce glass and top with a splash of Squirt. Garnish with mint sprig, if you like, and serve.

tequila tip

Fresca is a fine alternative to Squirt, and if your preference is for a lighter cooler with a tarter flavor, you can also make a version using silver tequila and regular grapefruit juice.

nueva cantina

Tex-Mex Martini

In this surprisingly smooth and civil cocktail, you will be completely seduced by the fragrance of cilantro, paired with that other Southwest favorite, tequila. Shaken vigorously, the combination of fiery silver tequila and lemon and lime releases the herb's intensity, letting its heady flavor sing from here to Guadalajara.

- 6 ice cubes
- 2 ounces silver tequila
- 6 to 8 fresh cilantro leaves
- 2½ ounces Sweet and Sour (recipe below)
- 1 tablespoon superfine sugar

Put the ice in a cocktail shaker and add the tequila, cilantro, Sweet and Sour, and sugar. Shake vigorously to blend and chill.

Pour the mixture, ice and all, into a tall 8-ounce glass and serve.

Sweet and Sour

There's nothing better than a great homemade sweet and sour mix. A classic base for many cocktails, this quickly covers both your sweet and citrus flavor needs, and the fresh juices bring up the quality way beyond those store-bought mutations. Make up a batch to have on hand, this recipe will yield enough for about 10 drinks, and you can always multiply for a crowd.

- 1 cup water
- 1 cup sugar
- ¾ cup fresh lime juice
- ¾ cup fresh lemon juice

In a small saucepan, bring the water to a boil. Add the sugar and stir slowly until dissolved. Reduce the heat to low and let simmer for 5 minutes. Remove from the heat, and let cool completely, about 30 minutes.

Pour the cooled sugar mixture into a clean glass jar, and add the lime juice and lemon juice. Cap tightly and shake contents until well-mixed.

Refrigerate until needed. This syrup will keep for up to 10 days.

Makes 2½ cups

Citrus Cantina Cooler

Tequila loves citrus! And for citrophiles who love both, this is the elixir of choice. Lemon, lime, grapefruit, and orange juices mix happily with a whisper of sweet almond from the orgeat syrup. Use silver tequila for a light, fresh flavor, or reposado tequila for a richer, warmer tone. A salt rim is optional.

1 lime wedge
¼ cup kosher salt in a small plate
1½ cups cracked ice, or 6 ice cubes
3 ounces tequila
1½ ounces fresh orange juice
1½ ounces fresh grapefruit juice
1 ounce fresh lime juice
1 ounce fresh lemon juice
3 ounces Sweet and Sour (Page 20)
1 ounce orgeat syrup

Garnish: 2 orange-peel spirals

Run the lime wedge around the rim of two 6-ounce cocktail glasses. Dip the moistened rims in the salt. Set the lime wedge aside and chill the glasses until ready to use.

Add the ice to a cocktail shaker, then add the tequila, juices, Sweet and Sour, and orgeat syrup. Shake vigorously to blend and chill.

Strain the mixture evenly between the 2 prepared glasses. Garnish each drink with a floating orange-peel spiral.

Mojave Mojito

The Cuban Mojito is one of the hottest drinks to hit the cocktail scene since the Cosmopolitan. Never being known as one to resist a bit of mixological tinkering, and with this rum drink beckoning loudly for a tequila conversion, I came up with a version that would convert Castro. So, you can either think of this as a Southern mint julep lost in the desert, or a Mojito taking a tequila holiday—whatever works for you. Just give this a test spin—I guarantee you won't be disappointed.

6 to 8 fresh spearmint leaves
1 tablespoon superfine sugar
1 ounce fresh lime juice
2 ounces silver tequila
6 ice cubes
2 ounces club soda

Garnish: 1 mint sprig

Put the mint, sugar, and lime juice in a tall 6-ounce glass. Using a muddler or the back of a bar spoon, muddle the contents together until the mint is crushed and the sugar is dissolved.

Add the tequila and stir to combine. Fill the glass with ice and add the club soda.

Stir to blend, garnish with the mint sprig, and serve.

Tijuana Taxi

Sidecars have been one of my personal favorites from way back. This version takes the classic Sidecar on one wild ride. I've used tequila in place of the usual brandy, and lots of sweet fresh tangerine juice instead of lemon juice. If tangerines aren't readily available, fresh orange juice is a fine substitute. Traditionalists can rim the glass with superfine sugar or, for that extra tang, a salt and lemon-zest rim.

6 ice cubes

2 ounces reposado tequila

2 ounces fresh tangerine juice

1 ounce Sweet and Sour (page 20)

1 ounce Cointreau

Garnish: 1 tangerine wheel (optional)

Chill a 6-ounce cocktail glass.

Add the ice to a cocktail shaker, then add the tequila, tangerine juice, Sweet and Sour, and Cointreau. Shake vigorously to blend and chill.

Pour the mixture into the chilled glass. Garnish the rim of the glass with the tangerine wheel, if you like, and serve.

tequila tip

For those who prefer a refreshingly tart ride, use the traditional ingredient of fresh lemon juice in place of tangerine juice.

Avocado Colada

This drink may make it seem like I've gone vegan (please—I'm from Texas), but you will just have to trust me on this one. Surprisingly awesome and luscious, rich and creamy, this light celadon green avocado cocktail has a lightly sweet flavor, citrus tones of lemon and lime, and fiery tones of silver tequila. Best made with a perfectly ripe avocado, it tastes like a creamy shake. Perfect for Sunday brunch on the patio.

4 to 5 ice cubes

1½ ounces silver tequila

1 ounce fresh lime juice

½ ounce fresh lemon juice

⅓ cup diced ripe avocado

1 ounce half-and-half

1 tablespoon superfine sugar

Garnish: 1 lime wheel,
1 avocado slice

Chill a 6-ounce cocktail glass.

In a blender, combine the ice, tequila, lime juice, lemon juice, avocado, half-and-half, and sugar. Blend until well combined and smooth.

Pour into the chilled glass. Using a cocktail pick, skewer the lime wheel and avocado slice together, place on the rim of the glass, and serve.

Tequila Gelatin Shooters

Gelatin shooters are hot! There's a huge wave of creative gelatin mixology going on right now; it's the latest in the quest for the quick and the potent. Colorful little jiggly cubes of your favorite gelatin fruit flavors are infused with any liquor of choice then tossed back shot-style as you enjoy the intensity of tastes on your tongue. Once you get the basics down, you can turn just about any favorite cocktail into a gelatin shooter.

The formula is pretty straightforward: Substitute a liquor of choice for half of the water called for in the recipe on a box of gelatin. Each recipe makes 20 gelatin shots, 2 or 3 per reveler, and you're there, baby! So serve a batch of these rowdy shooters at your next party to really liven things up.

The Pink Fix

Here's the sophisticated Cosmo, made with tequila instead of vodka, and the usual suspects of Grand Marnier, and lime juice, but tarted up with cranberry gelatin instead of the juice. This is sure to quickly fulfill your desire for this classic cocktail—and leave you feeling in the pink!

1 cup water

1 box (3 ounces) cranberry gelatin

4 ounces tequila

2 ounces Grand Marnier

2 ounces fresh lime juice

Garnish: 20 lemon-peel twists

In a small saucepan, bring the water to a boil. Pour the cranberry gelatin into a medium heatproof bowl. Stir in the boiling water, and continue stirring until the gelatin is dissolved. Let cool.

Add the tequila, Grand Marnier, and lime juice to the cooled mixture, stirring until well combined.

Divide the mixture among twenty 2-ounce paper or plastic cups and refrigerate until firm, 4 to 6 hours.

Garnish each cup by pushing a lemon twist into the gelatin and serve.

tequila tip

Purely for the decadence, try Very-berrylicious Tequila (page 93) in place of the straight stuff, for a berry flavor boost.

Sunshot

This is my homage to the Tequila Sunrise—in a jiggly sort of way. It's a stratified shooter in pink and orange layers of gelatin. (Oh-so-fun and innocent looking!) In one layer you have the tequila, Triple Sec, and tangy orange gelatin, and, for the traditional fizz factor, there's a second layer of sparkling wildberry gelatin and club soda. The layering method is simple: Just chill the first layer until set (but not completely firm) before adding the next layer. I will only warn you once; these luscious little numbers pack quite a wallop, so don't think you can inhale the whole batch yourself.

First Layer:
¾ cup water
1 box (3 ounces) orange gelatin
4 ounces tequila
2 ounces Triple Sec

Second Layer:
1 cup water
1 box (6 ounces) sparkling wildberry gelatin
1 cup club soda

To make the first layer: In a small saucepan, bring water to a boil. Pour the orange gelatin into a medium heatproof bowl. Stir in the boiling water, and continue stirring until the gelatin is dissolved. Let cool.

Add the tequila and Triple Sec to the cooled mixture, stirring until well combined.

Spoon 2 tablespoons of the orange gelatin mixture into each of thirty 2-ounce paper or plastic cups. Refrigerate till slightly set, about 30 minutes.

To make the second layer: In a small saucepan, bring the water to a boil.

Pour the sparkling wildberry gelatin into a medium heatproof bowl. Stir in the boiling water and continue stirring until the gelatin is dissolved. Let cool.

Add the club soda to the cooled mixture, stirring until well combined.

Spoon 2 tablespoons of the wildberry gelatin mixture into each of the cups of orange gelatin mixture. Refrigerate and chill until firm, 3 to 4 hours.

tequila tip

Try this with flavored sparkling waters, such as lemon or lime, in place of the club soda.

Gela-rita

This is pure perfection, a margarita compacted into one little jiggly shooter. Who could ask for more? Infused in the lime gelatin are tequila, lime juice, and Cointreau—all the essentials for a great margi. If you feel inspired to get authentic, wet the rims of the cups with a lime wedge and dip the moistened rims in a small plate of kosher salt before filling with the Gela-rita mixture.

1 cup water

1 box (3 ounces) lime gelatin

5 ounces tequila

2 ounces Cointreau

1 ounce fresh lime juice

In a small saucepan, bring the water to a boil.

Pour the lime gelatin into a medium heatproof bowl. Stir in the boiling water and continue stirring until the gelatin is dissolved. Let cool.

Add the tequila, Cointreau, and lime juice to the cooled mixture, stirring until well combined.

Divide the mixture among twenty 2-ounce paper or plastic cups, and refrigerate until firm, 4 to 6 hours.

tequila tip

Use strawberry gelatin in place of the lime gelatin for a great strawberry margarita shooter.

back porch quenchers

Nectarine Dream

Ripe nectarines, one of my favorite summer fruits, lend perfect lusciousness to this pitcher of *agua fresca*, the classic Mexican fruit-
based thirst quencher. This drink is normally not made with alcohol,
but I just couldn't resist a few splashes of tequila for torque, along
with tart fresh lime juice. Traditionally, *agua fresca* is made by blend-
ing fresh fruit and water to a smooth purée, which is strained through
a fine sieve into a pitcher. I have skipped this step, finding that the
pulp of the fruit adds richness to the drink, but you may prefer the
classic method. Ideally, this drink should be served right away, but
you can also pour the mixture into a glass pitcher and chill until you
are ready to serve, being sure to stir the contents before you do so.
Who knows? After your guests have had a few pitchers of these juicy,
potent elixirs, things might just spin into some crazy, magical
Midsummer Night's Dream scenario.

2 cups cold water

2 cups sliced peeled nectarines (about 4 nectarines)

1 cup silver tequila

½ cup fresh lime juice

¼ cup superfine sugar

1½ cups cracked ice

Garnish: 6 nectarine slices,

6 lime slices,

18 raspberries (optional),

6 mint sprigs (optional)

Chill 6 large margarita or cocktail glasses.

In a blender, in batches if necessary, combine the water, nectarines,
tequila, lime juice, sugar, and ice. Blend until completely smooth.

Divide the mixture evenly among the chilled glasses. Garnish each rim
with a nectarine slice and a lime slice, and serve. If you like, add 3
raspberries and a mint sprig to each glass for a touch of visual color.

tequila tip

Omit the tequila, and you have a great nonalcoholic
thirst quencher. Try substituting another fruit—such
as pineapple, peaches, or strawberries—for the
nectarines, or try papaya or mango.

Rancho-rita Deluxe

In the realm of adventurous margaritas, this one truly gilds the lily. It's a great excuse to round up your favorite revelers for a patio party. A pitcher of fresh juices blended with frosty pineapple sorbet, with the added luxe of Galliano liqueur replacing the usual Triple Sec with a surprising hint of licorice-vanilla flavors. I prefer this drink with the warmth of a reposado or añejo tequila, but silver (or blanco) is equally fine. Pineapple sorbet is ideal for a smoothie-like consistency, but pineapple-juice ice cubes will work in a pinch. Just freeze pineapple juice in an ice cube tray and substitute for the sorbet.

1 cup cracked ice

1 cup reposado or añejo tequila

1 cup fresh orange juice

¾ cup pineapple sorbet or pineapple juice

3 ounces fresh lime juice

2½ ounces Galliano liqueur

Garnish: 4 lime wheels,
4 pineapple slices

Chill 4 large margarita or cocktail glasses.

In a blender, combine the ice, tequila, orange juice, pineapple sorbet, lime juice, and Galliano. Blend until well combined and smooth.

Divide the blended mixture evenly among the 4 chilled glasses.

Skewer a lime wheel and a pineapple slice with a cocktail pick and place on the rim of a glass. Repeat the process for the remaining drinks and serve.

Cuatro Amigos Liquados

Tequila and citrus have always been great *compadres*, which makes this concoction a veritable party with its decadent abundance of three different citrus juices. I've also thrown the fruity zing of fresh raspberries into this traditional drink of fruit, honey, and milk. If fresh raspberries are out of season, frozen berries are a fine substitute.

4 ounces silver tequila

1½ cups fresh or frozen unsweetened raspberries

1½ cups crushed ice, or 6 ice cubes

½ ounce fresh lime juice

½ ounce fresh lemon juice

½ ounce fresh orange juice

¼ cup honey

¼ cup half-and-half

Garnish: 2 fresh mint sprigs

In a blender, combine all the ingredients except the garnish and purée until smooth.

Divide the mixture evenly between 2 tall glasses and garnish each with 1 mint sprig.

tequila tip

Add a sliced banana or 1 cup fresh chopped pineapple and a few fresh mint leaves to this drink for a super smoothie. For the classic nonalcoholic liquado, just omit the tequila.

Mexican Sno-cones
(Raspas)

My ongoing midlife crisis has motivated my mixological creativity in strange and wondrous ways. When I tapped into my youthful summer pursuit of perfectly sculpted frosty domes of pulverized ice with super-sweet Day-Glo-hued syrups and paired it with my equally zealous quest for a great tequila cocktail—voilá!—I came up with an adult-fantasy sno-cone!

I prefer to fulfill that intense, sweet hit of fruity flavor with frozen juice concentrates. They have a fresher taste than the syrupy sweet stuff that's usually poured on sno-cones. Look for concentrates with a high percentage of actual juice. And if you really must go vintage, Italian syrups in various flavors are a quick route to sweet intensity.

Instead of serving these frozen cocktails in the usual sno-cone paper cups, add a bit of swank and serve them in chilled martini or cocktail glasses, piling the ice high into a dome.

So, whether the ice cometh perfectly pulverized from an electric shave ice machine, hand cranked into big crunchy chunks by a metal ice crusher, or scraped with a spoon from a pan of frozen sugar water (very vintage), these high-octane Mexican sno-cones are the ultimate in fun. As one of the best quick summer cooldowns, they are guaranteed to lower your temperature on 100° days.

La Piña Coolada

It just doesn't get any better than this! My tropical rendition of a snowball in paradise is loosely based on the Piña Colada, made with tequila, pineapple juice, fresh lime juice (or thawed frozen limeade—your choice) and Thai coconut milk. This recipe can be multiplied to serve a crowd. If you chose to go with the limeade, a 12-ounce can of frozen concentrate is enough to make 12 sno-cones.

Garnish each glass or cup with a tiny purple orchid, and your guests will be crooning "Bali Ha'i" before you know it.

1 cup finely crushed sno-cone ice
1 ounce thawed frozen pineapple juice concentrate
1 ounce tequila
½ ounce fresh lime juice (or limeade)
½ ounce Thai coconut milk

Garnish: 1 small purple orchid

Chill a 6-ounce cocktail glass (optional), or choose a paper cup.

With a large spoon, carefully pack the crushed ice into the glass or cup.

In a small bowl, combine the pineapple juice concentrate, tequila, lime juice, and coconut milk. Stir until well blended.

Gradually pour the liquid mixture over the sno-cone ice. Garnish the sno-cone by gently pushing the stem of the orchid into the ice and serve.

tequila tip

For a great multiflavored substitute for pineapple juice concentrate, try a frozen tropical juice concentrate medley such as pineapple, orange, and banana.

Iced Pucker

Serious green apple lovers (and I do mean serious) will want to pucker up for this full-on apple-green tequila ice, with the flavor of Apple Pucker liqueur, limeade, and a fiery shot of tequila. As far as apple liqueurs go, either 99 Apples or Apple Pucker will be great in this recipe, but only the latter will give your sno-cone that extraordinary, otherworldly green hue.

1 cup finely crushed sno-cone ice
1 ounce thawed frozen limeade concentrate
1 ounce tequila
¾ ounce Sour Apple Pucker Schnapps

Garnish: 1 lime-peel twist

Chill a 6-ounce cocktail glass (optional), or choose a paper cup.

With a large spoon, carefully pack the crushed ice into the glass or cup.

In a small bowl, combine the limeade concentrate, tequila, and liqueur. Stir until well blended.

Gradually pour the liquid mixture over the sno-cone ice. Garnish the sno-cone by gently pushing the end of the lime peel into the ice and serve.

Icy Bluecaracha

At first glance, this may appear to be one of those innocent screaming-Windex-blue sno-cones. But this gem takes the classic blue sno-cone to a whole other level, compliments of blue curaçao, along with tangy lemonade and a very adult tequila kick.

1 cup finely crushed sno-cone ice
1 ounce thawed frozen lemonade concentrate
1 ounce tequila
¾ ounce blue curaçao

Garnish: 1 small pink orchid,
1 lemon peel

Chill a 6-ounce cocktail glass (optional), or choose a paper cup.

With a large spoon, carefully pack the crushed ice into the glass or cup.

In a small bowl, combine the lemonade concentrate, tequila, and blue curaçao. Stir until well blended.

Gradually pour the liquid mixture over the sno-cone ice. Garnish by gently pushing the stem of the orchid and the end of the lemon peel into the ice and serve.

tequila tip

 Add a splash of raspberry syrup on top for the ultimate in decadence.

Orangesicle

This combo is pure frozen sunshine: citrusy orange (or tangerine) juice, tequila, and Grand Marnier. This recipe has both fresh and frozen juice for a good sweet-tart balance. I highly recommend tangerine juice as a tangy departure from the usual orange juice. Again, you can multiply this recipe for a crowd, measuring out 2½ ounces of the mixture per sno-cone.

1 to 1½ cups finely crushed sno-cone ice
1 ounce thawed frozen orange
    or tangerine juice concentrate
½ ounce fresh orange or tangerine juice
1 ounce tequila
½ ounce Grand Marnier

Garnish: 1 mint sprig

Chill a 6-ounce cocktail glass (optional), or choose a paper cup.

With a large spoon, carefully pack the crushed ice into the glass or cup.

In a small bowl, combine the juice concentrate, fresh juice, tequila, and Grand Marnier. Stir until well blended.

Gradually pour the liquid mixture over the sno-cone ice. Garnish by gently pushing the stem of the mint sprig into the ice and serve.

tequila tip

Try this recipe using a guava–passion fruit–orange juice concentrate in place of the orange juice concentrate. Fabulous!

Tequila Tangrita

This effervescent and potent concoction is made, sangría-style, with a fruity mixture of sliced green apples, oranges, and lemons, spiked with tequila, Triple Sec, brandy, and the spicy tones of clove—all happily suspended in sparkling apple-cranberry cider (such as Martinelli's). This drink only gets better over time. You can prepare a pitcher the day before your soirée, leaving the fruit and alcohol mixture in the refrigerator overnight. The longer the fruit macerates in the liquid, the more flavorful the punch. Stir in the sparkling cider just before serving. It's ideal for patio brunches, and I strongly suggest you make a few backup pitchers, just in case—these go fast.

2 green apples, cored and sliced

1 tangerine or small orange, quartered and sliced

1 lemon, quartered and sliced

15 cloves

2 ounces fresh lemon juice

2 ounces fresh lime juice

2 ounces Triple Sec

½ cup brandy

1½ cups tequila

2 bottles (750 ml each) sparkling apple-cranberry cider

6 cups ice cubes (about 3 ice cube trays)

Garnish: 8 to 10 mint sprigs

In a large (at least 8 cups) glass pitcher, combine the fruit and sprinkle in the whole cloves. Add the lemon juice, lime juice, Triple Sec, brandy, and tequila stirring gently to combine.

Refrigerate the mixture for at least 1 hour, or preferably 2 to 12 hours, to infuse the liquid with the fruit and spice flavors and to chill.

To serve, add the sparkling apple-cranberry cider to the chilled mixture in the pitcher and stir to combine.

Fill 8 to 10 large (10-ounce) tall glasses or wine goblets with the ice cubes. Add the cider mixture, making sure each drink gets some of the marinated fruit. Garnish each drink with a mint sprig and serve.

---

tequila tip

Add 1 cup fresh or thawed frozen unsweetened raspberries and blueberries to the mix, and use Very-berrylicious Tequila (page 93)—for a real blast of berry flavor.

Stumbling Tumbleweed Punch

I'm absolutely serious about the name, so don't let the innocent pink hue and the aromatic play of sweet black currants and ginger on your tongue fool you, this is one feisty punch. It has so much zing, it will put the fizz in your next backyard bash. This recipe serves five to six revelers, about 4½ cups per batch. If you have a larger crowd, make it in batches ahead of time in the blender, minus the ginger ale. Transfer to glass pitchers and chill in the refrigerator. When ready to serve, stir in the ginger ale (or my fave, spicy ginger beer).

6 ice cubes, plus more for glasses
6 ounces (½ can) frozen limeade concentrate
3 ounces fresh lime juice
1 cup cold water
1 cup tequila
½ cup crème de cassis
1 cup ginger ale or ginger beer

Garnish: 5 to 6 lime wedges

In a blender, combine the 6 ice cubes, the limeade, lime juice, water, tequila, and crème de cassis. Blend until well combined and slushy. Add the ginger ale and blend on low speed for a few seconds.

Fill 6 tall glasses with ice cubes and divide the liquid mixture evenly among the glasses. Squeeze a lime wedge into each drink, dropping in the wedges, and serve.

tequila tip

Float a few slices of lemons, limes, and oranges in your pitcher of punch; it looks great and will intensify the citrus flavors.

el aperitivo nacional

Mango Pellegringo

I've decided that mangos are definitely the fruit of the gods—flavorful and intense, sweet and juicy—and therefore this would be their perfect brunch cocktail: fresh mango purée, tequila, and a splash of fresh orange juice, whirled together and topped with prosecco (Italian sparkling wine). Fresh mango is ideal, but frozen mango is a fine substitute, and available in most supermarkets. Add the prosecco to taste; the more you add the lighter the drink, and the less thick and smoothie-like.

1 ounce silver tequila
½ cup cubed ripe mango
1 ounce fresh orange juice
4 to 6 ounces chilled prosecco

Garnish: 4 mango slices,
2 lime slices

Chill two 6-ounce champagne flutes or tall, thin highball glasses.

In a blender, combine the tequila, mango, and orange juice. Blend until well combined and smooth.

Divide the blended mixture evenly between the chilled glasses. Gradually pour in the prosecco, topping each glass. Skewer 2 mango slices and 1 lime slice with a cocktail pick. Place one on the rim of each glass and serve.

tequila tip

For those who simply cannot get enough fruit in their, ahem, diet, the addition of a few sliced fresh or frozen strawberries puts this cocktail into a fruity pink realm.

Limonada Blanca

Once you've had a cocktail made with limoncello, your mind reels with all the puckery possibilities. This light and bubbly apéritif satisfies the desire to suck on a lemon, in a good way. Silver tequila and tart fresh lemon juice are perfectly balanced with the lemony-sweet addition of Italian limoncello liqueur, for one shimmery, refined cocktail.

6 ice cubes

2 ounces silver tequila

1 ounce limoncello liqueur

1½ ounces fresh lemon juice

1 teaspoon superfine sugar

Splash of club soda

Garnish: 1 mint sprig (optional)

Fill a cocktail shaker with the ice. Add the tequila, limoncello, lemon juice, and sugar. Shake vigorously to blend and chill.

Pour the entire shaker contents, including the ice, into a 6-ounce highball glass. Top with club soda, garnish with the mint sprig, if you like, and serve.

Campesino Quencher

For those who love Campari but are looking for a *nuevo* way to enjoy the bittersweet ruby-hued Italian classic, this swank cooler is it. Matched with the fire of tequila and tart but sweet pink grapefruit, Campari adds that extra refining note. A splash of club soda makes for a refreshingly tart *aperitivo*.

6 ice cubes

1½ ounces silver tequila

2 ounces fresh pink grapefruit juice

½ ounce Campari

2 to 3 ounces club soda

Garnish: 1 lemon-peel twist

Chill a 6-ounce highball glass.

Fill a cocktail shaker with the ice. Add the tequila, grapefruit juice, and Campari. Shake vigorously to blend and chill.

Pour the entire contents of the shaker, ice and all, into the highball glass, and top with club soda. Twist the lemon peel over the drink, then drop it into the drink and serve.

Damiana Diabla

We're playing with fire here: a thoroughly enjoyable combination of notorious tequila and naughty Damiana liqueur, that sultry aphrodisiac from Baja. Muddled with fresh lime wedges, Caipirinha style, they make a refreshing thirst quencher that may just have you bargaining with the Horned One.

4 or 5 lime wedges

1 tablespoon superfine sugar

1 cup cracked ice

2 ounces tequila

1 ounce Damiana liqueur

Put the lime wedge into an old-fashioned glass and sprinkle the sugar over the limes.

Using a muddler or the back of a bar spoon, muddle the sugar and limes together until the sugar is dissolved and the lime juice is released.

Add the cracked ice and pour in the tequila and liqueur. Stir a few revolutions and serve.

tequila tip

Try this with a few orange wedges and honey instead of lime and sugar for warmer flavor tone.

Ginger-Melon Snap

Watermelon has the undeniably juicy sweet flavor of summer, and when you add the unexpected snappy spice of ginger-infused silver tequila to the equation, you have one tall, slushy cooler. Now, if the ginger tequila's Asian intonations don't leave your friends completely wowed during your next front-porch cocktail hour, just grate a bit of fragrant fresh ginger into their drink and watch the mouths drop in foodie adulation. For an extra-thick and frosty drink, freeze the watermelon cubes.

3 ounces Spicy Ginger-Infused Tequila (page 96)

1½ cups diced seeded watermelon

2 ounces fresh lime juice

1 ounce fresh lemon juice

1 tablespoon grated fresh ginger

1 tablespoon honey

10 to 12 ice cubes

Garnish: 2 candied ginger slices, or 2 lemon wheels, 2 watermelon slices

In a blender, combine the tequila, watermelon, lime juice, lemon juice, ginger, and honey. Blend until well combined and the watermelon is puréed.

Fill 2 tall 10-ounce glasses with the ice cubes and divide the mixture evenly between the glasses. Garnish and serve.

Pear o' Snake Eyes

Pear brandy is one of those sneaky liquors, as it has a fiery afterbite to its fragrant pear flavor. Add ambrosial apricot nectar and a pleasantly tart razzle of fresh grapefruit juice, and you have a delicious balance of fruit and fire. If you can find it, I highly recommend using real grenadine made with pomegranate juice.

1½ cups cracked ice, or 6 ice cubes

2 ounces silver tequila

1 ounce pear brandy

4 ounces pink grapefruit juice

4 ounces apricot nectar

Splash of grenadine

Garnish: 2 thin pink grapefruit slices,
white cranberries (optional)

Chill two 6-ounce cocktail glasses.

Fill a cocktail shaker with the ice and add all the ingredients except the garnish. Shake vigorously to blend and chill.

Strain the mixture evenly between the 2 chilled glasses. Garnish the rim of each glass with a pink grapefruit slice and white cranberries, if you like, and serve.

Cucarumba

There's nothing like the crisp, clean taste of cucumbers. In a frothy blended cocktail, they have amazing transformational properties, turning your drink into a light and refreshing ambrosia. Hey, the English know what they're doing when they pair cukes with Champagne, so why not with tequila? (I prefer an añejo tequila for its spicy warmth, although silver tequila brings its own equally fine spark.) Together with the orange tones of Cointreau, tequila imparts a rich dimension to the light, fresh cucumber. Again, the best cucumbers to use are the long, thin English (hothouse) ones: great flavor, with practically non-existent seeds.

2 cups crushed ice, or 8 ice cubes

¾ cup diced peeled cucumber

3 ounces tequila

2 ounces Cointreau

3 ounces fresh lime juice

1 tablespoon superfine sugar

Garnish: 2 lime wedges

Chill two 6-ounce cocktail glasses.

Put the ice in a blender and add the cucumber, tequila, Cointreau, lime juice, and sugar. Blend until well combined and slushy.

Divide the blended mixture evenly between the chilled glasses. Squeeze a lime wedge into each glass, drop the wedge into the glass, and serve.

tequila tip

For a fabulously fruity twist, add ½ cup fresh or ½ cup frozen unsweetened raspberries to the mix.

tropiquila

Congarita

This tropical version of the margarita is so relaxed, it has tipped over into Mai Tai land! The basic margi elements of lime juice, Cointreau, and mellow reposado tequila are in place. From there it takes an island departure into fresh sweet pineapple and a whisper of banana (crème de banane), along with zingy lemon and orange juice. Don't be afraid to go all out—garnish galore!

3 ounces reposado tequila

2 ounces Cointreau

1 ounce crème de banane

2 tablespoons superfine sugar

2 ounces fresh lime juice

2 ounces fresh lemon juice

1 ounce fresh orange juice

1 cup fresh pineapple chunks

1½ cups cracked ice

Garnish: Lime zest

Chill two 8-ounce margarita glasses or cocktail glasses.

In a blender, combine the tequila, Cointreau, crème de banane, sugar, and juices. Blend for a few seconds. Add the pineapple chunks and the ice. Blend until well combined and smooth.

Divide the blended mixture evenly between the 2 chilled glasses.

Top each drink with a pinch of lime zest.

Tiki Tequila-a-Go-Go

Did I mention something about mango being the fruit of the gods? The tiki gods, that is. Fresh mango purée and coconut syrup pair up for this potent cocktail, which is shaken with a splash of Grand Marnier and lime juice to give it a hint of respectability and urban chic. Coconut syrup can be found at any market carrying Italian syrups, typically found in the coffee section. A spoonful of cream of coconut (such as Coco Lopez) is a yummy alternative if you have trouble finding the coconut syrup.

6 ice cubes

4 ounces silver tequila

1 cup cubed mango

1 ounce coconut syrup

2 ounces Grand Marnier

2 ounces fresh lime juice

Garnish: 2 lime wheels,
2 mango slices,
2 cranberries

Chill two 8-ounce cocktail glasses.

In a blender, combine the ice, tequila, mango, coconut syrup, Grand Marnier, and lime juice. Blend until the mango is puréed and the ingredients are well combined and slushy.

Divide the blended mixture evenly between the 2 chilled glasses.

Skewer 1 lime wheel and 1 mango slice together on a cocktail pick topped with a cranberry and place on the rim of a glass. Repeat for the second glass and serve.

Midori Matador

Midori, the Japanese liqueur notorious for its vibrant green hue, has a delicately sweet muskmelon flavor that only slightly tames the *toro* of silver tequila. The orange tones of Triple Sec and a splash of fresh lemon juice lend a citrusy balance to this tall, neon-green cooler.

1½ cups cracked ice, or 6 ice cubes

3 ounces Midori liqueur

2 ounces silver tequila

1 ounce Triple Sec

3 ounces fresh lemon juice

2 tablespoons superfine sugar

10 to 12 ice cubes

Garnish: 2 lemon wedges

Fill a cocktail shaker with the ice and add the Midori, tequila, Triple Sec, lemon juice, and sugar. Shake vigorously to blend and chill.

Fill two 8-ounce glasses with the ice cubes. Strain the mixture evenly between the glasses. Squeeze a lemon wedge into each drink and drop the wedge into the glass. Serve.

tequila tip

For a "swank and urbane" variation, try shaken and served "up."

Blue Agave

Let your tequila ride a new wave of lush island flavors straight into this aquamarine-hued tropical cocktail made with Thai coconut milk, sweet orange-flavoring from curaçao and the almond whisper of orgeat syrup. Look for canned Thai coconut milk in the ethnic-food section of your supermarket.

1½ cups cracked ice, or 6 ice cubes
3 ounces tequila
2 ounces blue curaçao
2 ounces Thai coconut milk
1½ ounces fresh lime juice
1 ounce orgeat syrup
1 tablespoon superfine sugar

Garnish: 2 mint sprigs,
2 orange slices

Chill two 6-ounce cocktail glasses.

Fill a cocktail shaker with the ice and add all the ingredients except the garnish. Shake vigorously to blend and chill.

Strain the mixture evenly between the 2 chilled glasses.

Garnish each rim with a mint sprig–studded orange slice and serve.

Feisty Jamaican Splash

Mint julep meets *iaye, caramba!* in this sparkling drink that goes
down as smooth and refreshing as a southern breeze, and as lively
as a gyrating conga line. Visually alluring, with fresh mint, it has
the effervescent extra-spicy kick of Jamaican ginger beer, an intense-
flavored premium ginger ale found in many natural foods stores.

1½ ounces fresh lemon juice

6 to 8 fresh spearmint leaves

1 teaspoon superfine sugar

1½ ounces tequila

6 ice cubes

Splash of ginger beer

Garnish: 1 mint sprig

Chill an 8-ounce highball glass.

In the chilled glass, combine the lemon juice, mint leaves, and sugar.
Muddle them together with a muddler or the back of a bar spoon until
the sugar dissolves and the mint is crushed.

Add the tequila and stir to blend. Add the ice and top with ginger
beer. Drop a mint sprig on top for garnish and serve.

Iguanabanana

This frosty frozen concoction has fresh bananas, 99 Bananas liqueur, a spritz of lime, and the frozen zing factor of lemon sorbet, along with the sharp bite of tequila to keep them all in line. Whether you're a big bananaphile or not, you'll dig this drink—*Iguanabanana*, baby!

2 cups crushed ice, or 8 to 10 ice cubes

3 ounces tequila

1 ounce fresh lime juice

1 ounce 99 Bananas liqueur or crème de banane

1/4 cup lemon sorbet

1 ripe banana, peeled and sliced

Garnish: 2 small purple orchids

Chill two 6-ounce cocktail glasses.

In a blender, combine all the ingredients and blend until slushy.

Divide the mixture evenly between the 2 chilled glasses, garnish each with an orchid, and serve.

Guava-Peach Passion

This drink will spark your passion for sand beneath your toes on some lush tropical beach—but if you can't get there, just sip a few of these and dip your toes in a plastic kiddy pool (it's much easier to find dropped garnishes that way). If you can't find Alize at your local liquor store, try surfing the Web; there are several sites you can order from.

3 ounces tequila

2 ounces Alize passion fruit liqueur

1/2 cup diced peeled fresh peach (about 1 peach)

1/2 cup lemon sorbet or gelato

3/4 cup guava nectar or juice

1/2 cup crushed ice

Garnish: 2 lemon wheels,
Dusting of ground nutmeg

In a blender, combine all the ingredients and blend until well combined and smooth.

Divide the mixture evenly between 2 tall 8-ounce glasses. Garnish the rim of each glass with a lemon wheel and nutmeg and serve.

dulce vida

Beauty and the Beast

You simply cannot get more decadent than this! The richness of chocolate and the liquid fire of tequila, sparked with fresh citrus juices—what could be more fulfilling? Okay, Godiva chocolate liqueur in place of crème de cacao will definitely push it right over the edge, but that's what we're after, isn't it?

6 ice cubes

1½ ounces silver tequila

1 ounce crème de cacao

½ ounce fresh lime juice

½ ounce fresh lemon juice

2 ounces fresh orange juice

Garnish: 1 lime wedge

Fill a cocktail shaker with the ice. Add the tequila, crème de cacao, lime juice, lemon juice, and orange juice. Shake vigorously to blend and chill.

Pour the mixture, ice and all, into a tall 6-ounce glass.

Squeeze the lime wedge over the top of the drink, drop the wedge into the drink, and serve.

tequila tip

For a refreshing spritzy cooler, try topping with a sparkling orange soda, such as San Pellegrino Aranciata or Orangina, in place of fresh orange juice. Or try whipping this concoction with ½ cup vanilla ice cream in a blender for a rich after-dinner drink. It can also be served "up" in a chilled tumbler.

Tijuana Speedball

This drink is sooo smooth and completely addictive. Created by the great innovative mixmistress Felicia Sledge at Blue Hour (a swank hotspot in Portland, Oregon) and thoroughly tested by me, again and again, it's made with the sweet java tones of Kahlúa and fueled by tequila and espresso, with Baileys Irish Cream to take the edge off. A fine dusting of cinnamon finished nicely with floating espresso beans, and you're energized to slow dance for hours.

6 ice cubes

½ ounce reposado tequila

½ ounce Kahlúa

½ ounce Baileys Irish Cream

1½ ounces espresso

Garnish: Dusting of cinnamon,
3 espresso beans

Chill a 6-ounce cocktail glass.

Fill a cocktail shaker with the ice. Add the tequila, Kahlúa, Baileys, and espresso. Shake vigorously to blend and chill.

Strain the mixture into the chilled cocktail glass. Sprinkle with a dusting of cinnamon and float the espresso beans on top. Serve.

Midnight Muchacho

A deliciously potent combination of tequila, Metaxa (Greek brandy), and Drambuie, with its sweet herb and honey tones, is blended together with vanilla ice cream and Mexican chocolate. My favorite Mexican chocolate is Ibarra, with its great spicy cinnamon flavor.

6 ice cubes

1½ ounces tequila

1 ounce Metaxa

1 ounce Drambuie

1 cup vanilla ice cream

¼ cup Mexican or dark chocolate shavings

Garnish: Mexican or dark chocolate shavings (optional)

Chill two 6-ounce cocktail glasses.

In a blender, combine the ice, tequila, Metaxa, Drambuie, ice cream, and ¼ cup chocolate shavings. Blend until smooth and creamy.

Divide the mixture evenly between the 2 chilled glasses. Garnish the top of each drink with a few chocolate shavings, if you like, and serve.

Noches Mexicanas

This is a great cocktail for late-night sipping, lulling you into a state of complete and utter bliss. Creamy and divine, with the rich warmth of reposado or añejo tequila and the complex, nutty tones of Frangelico liqueur, a bit of half-and-half, and a dusting of cinnamon (nutmeg is equally good) shaken and served up—*imuy elegante!*

1½ cups cracked ice

3 ounces reposado or añejo tequila

2 ounces half-and-half

1 ounce Frangelico liqueur

Garnish: Pinch of ground cinnamon

Chill 2 cocktail glasses or small snifters.

Fill a cocktail shaker with the ice. Add the tequila, half-and-half, and liqueur. Shake vigorously to blend and chill.

Strain the mixture evenly between the 2 chilled glasses. Sprinkle a pinch of cinnamon over the top of each and serve.

speedy gonzales

Cactus Hooch

Prickly pear juice is a natural *compadre* to agave. This amazingly fuchsia-colored, sweet cactus-fruit elixir is paired with tequila and a squeeze of lime, then shaken to a fizzy fury. This is a shot to hit your sweet spot. Look for prickly pear juice in specialty foods or Latino markets.

1 cup cracked ice

1½ ounces silver tequila

1 ounce prickly pear juice

Chill a tall 3-ounce shot glass or highball glass.

Fill a cocktail shaker with the ice. Add the tequila and prickly pear juice. Shake vigorously to blend and chill.

Strain the shaken mixture into the chilled glass. Gulp down or sip to savor.

tequila tip

Guava nectar (either canned or frozen concentrate) is another great juice to use in place of the prickly pear juice.

East by Southwest

In striving to create an urbane and swank version of the spicy-hot tequila shot, I came up with this minimal and elegant Pan-Asian combo: A perfect balance of wasabi (a pea-sized dab of that hot green Japanese horseradish paste will do ya), fresh ginger, and a premium silver tequila. It's a visually alluring and great-tasting hot shot.

$1/8$ teaspoon wasabi paste
$1/4$ teaspoon minced fresh ginger
$1 1/2$ ounces silver tequila
1 lime wedge

In a 2-ounce shot glass, combine the wasabi and ginger. Stir with a spoon or chopstick until well blended.

Add the tequila, stirring the mixture a few revolutions. Drink down the shot, then take a bite of the lime wedge.

Bite of the Chihuahua

Take the bite of fiery tequila, add the spicy herbal tones of green Chartreuse and lime juice, add a flaming float of 151-proof rum, and you have one potent shot that's just got to be more enjoyable than the real thing! (Not that I care to test this statement.)

1 cup cracked ice
1 ounce tequila
½ ounce fresh lime juice
½ ounce green Chartreuse
½ ounce 151-proof rum

Fill a cocktail shaker with the ice. Add the tequila, lime juice, and green Chartreuse. Shake vigorously to blend and chill.

Strain the mixture into a tall 3-ounce shot glass.

Very slowly pour the rum over the back of a spoon to float it on top of the drink.

Using a long match, carefully ignite the rum and let it burn for a few seconds. Blow out the flame and let the glass cool a bit before sipping or shooting.

tequila tip

Try substituting Galliano for green Chartreuse, for a bite of licorice-vanilla flavor.

Bull Shot

Savory, spicy, and Bloody Mary–esque, this variation on the classic bull shot is the perfect "hair of the dog" shot: a shaken concoction of puréed fresh tomatoes, beef bouillon (finding the best and freshest bouillon is key) and a little, or a lot, of the hot stuff, adjusted for personal perfection.

1 lime wedge
Kosher salt in a small plate
6 ice cubes
1½ ounces premium tequila
¼ cup tomato purée
3 ounces beef bouillon
1 or 2 dashes hot sauce (to taste)
Dash Worcestershire sauce
Pinch of freshly ground black pepper

Garnish: 1 lime wedge

Run the lime wedge around the rim of a 6-ounce highball glass. Dip the moistened rim in the salt. Set the lime wedge aside and chill the salted glass.

Fill a cocktail shaker with the ice. Add the tequila, tomato purée, beef bouillon, hot sauce, Worcestershire, and pepper. Shake vigorously to blend and chill.

Strain the mixture into the prepared glass, squeeze the lime wedge for garnish into the cocktail, and serve.

Redheaded Stranger

This seductive little layered sipping shot, with spicy salsa, pineapple purée, lime juice, and a good-quality tequila, will immediately become one of your favorites. The recipe serves one, but can be easily made for a crowd. Just purée one cup of diced fresh pineapple and a squeeze of fresh lime juice in a blender and layer a few shots all at once, lined up and ready for soon-to-be-very happy friends. A medium-hot fruity salsa made with peaches, mango, or pineapple is perfect for this shooter.

1 tablespoon medium-hot salsa
1 tablespoon pineapple purée
½ ounce fresh lime juice
1 ounce tequila
1 lime wedge

Chill a tall 3- or 4-ounce shot glass.

Drop the salsa into the chilled glass.

To create the next layer, slowly pour in the pineapple purée.

Gradually pour the lime juice over the back of a spoon into the drink, then repeat the process with the tequila.

Bite into the lime wedge and then sip away.

The Good, the Bad, and the Ugly

This is a layered shot that covers all the bases—it's your call which is good, bad, or ugly. The trick to layering different liquors is to pour the heaviest on the bottom and the lightest on top. Each is poured very slowly over the back of a spoon. From the bottom up, this one has coffee-flavored Kahlúa liqueur, sweet black raspberry–flavored Chambord, and silver tequila. Sip to decipher all the complex flavors, or slam it down.

1 lime wedge
½ ounce Kahlúa
½ ounce Chambord
½ ounce silver tequila

Run the lime wedge around the rim of a tall 2-ounce shot glass. Set the lime wedge aside and chill the glass.

Pour the Kahlúa into the prepared shot glass.

Pour the Chambord very gradually over the back of a spoon to make a second layer, floating it on top of the Kahlúa. Repeat the process with the tequila for a third layer. Shoot back, or sip and savor.

Tijuana Itch

Sate your thirst for the quickest margi this side of the border with a fiery shot of 100 percent agave silver tequila layered between fresh lime juice and a salt rim. This is an all-in-one compact shot based on the classic three-step Tres Amigos. And of course it wouldn't be complete without the quintessential Lone Star beer chaser (Corona *cerveza* or any pale ale is a fine substitute if Lone Star can't be found).

1 lime wedge
Kosher salt in a small plate
½ ounce fresh lime juice
1½ ounces silver tequila

Run the lime wedge around the rim of a tall 2-ounce shot glass. Dip the moistened rim in the salt. Set the lime aside.

Pour the lime juice, then the tequila, into the prepared glass. Gulp down the shot, take a bite of the lime wedge, and take a swig of beer.

infusion profusion

Tequila Infusions

I always have a bottle of tequila infusing away in the refrigerator or freezer with some luscious fruit, herb, or spice (and sometimes all together). It's a savvy shortcut to a complex flavor adventure, just waiting to be shared with friends as a divine sipping aperitif, or used in a favorite margarita recipe. The best tequila to use for infusions is a moderately priced silver, light, or white, given their mild flavor. But don't rule out a reposado or an añejo—they're a bit more expensive, but they make a sublime and sippable treat on the rocks with a splash of seltzer. For a real indulgence that cuts to the chase, I love to pour them straight over sno-cones.

Cuatro-Citrus Infusion

Infusing tequila with fragrant grapefruit, lime, lemon, and orange essence gives it that super-citrusy tequila tang and makes it a fabulous vehicle for cocktails. Typically, the stronger the essence of the added ingredient, the less time involved getting the desired taste; this one steeps for two days. This is such a versatile infusion, the list of its applications could go on and on, so I will limit it to a few suggestions such as Sparkling Sunrise Cooler (page 13) and, of course, almost any margarita. Or try it poured over a sno-cone for an instant summery cool treat.

1 bottle (750 ml) silver tequila
1 grapefruit
1 lime
1 lemon
1 orange

With a paring knife, cut the peel off each citrus fruit in long, thin strips.

Put the citrus peels in a 6-cup glass jar with a screw top. Add the tequila. Cover the jar tightly. Let sit in a cool, dark place for 48 hours, shaking the jar gently once or twice a day.

Taste for flavor; let steep for up to a week if you prefer stronger flavor.

Strain the steeped mixture through a fine-meshed sieve into a large bowl.

Using a funnel, pour the flavored tequila back into the original bottle and cap tightly. Label and refrigerate or freeze indefinitely for long-term storage.

Very-berrylicious Tequila

Infusing the fragrant essence from raspberries and blackberries into tequila gives it an intense fruity flavor dimension, just ripe for the mixing. Fresh berries are best, but you can also use thawed frozen unsweetened berries. Most fruits take about two weeks of macerating for the ultimate in flavor, but you can taste test as you go. Strawberries are easily substituted for either of the berries below.

1 bottle (750 ml) silver tequila
2 cups fresh raspberries
2 cups fresh blackberries

Put the fruit in a 6-cup glass jar with a screw top. Add the tequila. Cover tightly.

Let sit in a cool, dark place for 1½ weeks, shaking the jar gently every 2 to 3 days.

Taste for flavor. Let steep for 3 days longer if you prefer a stronger flavor.

Strain the steeped mixture through a fine-meshed sieve into a bowl. Reserve the berries, freezing them to make frozen margaritas later.

Using a funnel, pour the flavored tequila back into the original bottle and cap tightly. Label and refrigerate or freeze indefinitely for long-term storage.

tequila tip

Try this berry-infused tequila in your next margarita for a great fruity blast of flavor. It's also a sensational addition to a Nacionalista (page 15) and tailor-made for a Cuatro Amigos Liquados (page 37).

Tropical Tequila

This is one of my favorite recipes, with intense island flavors built right in and ready to splash straight into a Tiki Tequila-a-Go-Go (page 62). You can use a silver or reposado tequila, but I prefer an añejo, with it's warmth similar to a good Demerara rum. Slowly sipping this chilled elixir of tequila infused with mango, pineapple, and vanilla bean is a shortcut to tropical bliss. Using it in your next margarita will give you an instant tikirita—Ya, Mon!

2 cups cubed fresh pineapple
1 ripe mango, peeled, cut from pit, and cubed
3 vanilla beans, broken into small pieces
1 bottle (750 ml) tequila

In a 6-cup glass jar with a screw top, combine the pineapple, mango, and vanilla beans. Add the tequila and close tightly.

Let stand in a cool, dark place for 48 hours, shaking gently once or twice a day.

Refrigerate the mixture, shaking gently once a day for up to 1 week. Taste for flavor after 4 days.

Using a funnel and a fine-meshed sieve, strain the mixture into the original bottle. (Reserve the solids and freeze to use later in frozen margaritas.)

Cap tightly, label, and refrigerate or freeze indefinitely for long-term storage.

Tres Melones Galore

This infusion is a fabulous way to add a mucho melony twist to a frozen margarita and is perfect for those tall, spritzy coolers like Midori Matador (page 64). Or, use it with an Iced Pucker sno-cone (page 41) to add more depth of flavor.

1 cup fresh watermelon cubes
1 cup fresh cantaloupe cubes
1 cup fresh honeydew melon cubes
1 bottle (750 ml) good-quality silver tequila

Put the melons in a 6-cup glass jar with a screw top. Add the tequila and close tightly.

Let sit in a cool, dark place for 1 week.

Taste for flavor; let steep up to 3 days longer for a stronger flavor.

Using a funnel and a fine-meshed sieve lined with cheesecloth, strain the mixture back into the original bottle. Cap tightly, label, and refrigerate or freeze indefinitely for long-term storage.

Spicy Ginger-Infused Tequila

This refined infusion makes a sublime tequila martini and adds a spicy edge to cocktails. It's especially fine in Ginger-Melon Snap (page 55), lending that cocktail an awesome ginger-flavored boost.

1 bottle (750 ml) silver tequila
1 cup peeled, thinly sliced fresh ginger

Put the ginger in a 6-cup glass jar with a screw top. Add the tequila and close tightly.

Let sit in a cool, dark place for 48 hours, shaking gently once every day.

Taste for flavor; let steep for up to 4 days if you want a stronger flavor.

Using a funnel and a fine-meshed sieve, strain the mixture back into the original bottle, cap, and refrigerate or freeze indefinitely for long-term storage.

fiesta nibbles

Roasted Three-Pepper Salsa

As far as salsas go, we are definitely gilding the lily here. A Mexican festival of flavors come together in sweet harmony, with multicolored bell peppers, ripe tomatoes, and jalapeno peppers, all rolled into one robust, beautiful salsa. I definitely recommend you grill all the ingredients first, to infuse the peppers with that great flame-roasted taste. This is not only a great dipping salsa, it's also excellent as a topping for fajitas or stirred into guacamole. And if you're lucky enough to have any left over, it's great in scrambled eggs the next day.

1 yellow bell pepper

1 red bell pepper

½ white onion

1 teaspoon extra-virgin olive oil

4 unpeeled cloves garlic

2 cups chopped tomatoes

½ cup minced fresh cilantro

2 jalapeño peppers, minced

4 teaspoons fresh lime juice

1 teaspoon salt

Preheat the broiler. Cut the bell peppers in half lengthwise; remove the stems and seeds. Place, cut-side down, on a baking sheet lined with aluminum foil. Flatten with the palm of your hand. Cut the onion into large chunks; toss with the olive oil. Put the onion and garlic on the baking sheet. Broil 3 inches from the heat, stirring every few minutes, until the onion starts to brown (don't let it burn). Remove the garlic cloves when softened. Broil the bell peppers until the skins are blackened. Transfer to a paper bag, seal, and let steam for 10 minutes to loosen the skins. Remove and discard the skins; chop the bell peppers. Peel the garlic cloves and mince. Chop the onion. Combine the bell peppers, onion, garlic, tomatoes, cilantro, jalapeños, lime juice, and salt in a bowl. Cover and refrigerate for 1 to 2 hours to blend the flavors.

hot tip

Prepare the bell peppers, onion, and garlic a day ahead, cover, and refrigerate.

Killer Guacamole

The deceptively simple combination of avocado blended with the spicy, feisty *compadres* of onion, garlic, jalapenos, and tomatoes makes a sublime guac. When you serve it with a frosty margarita, the way I see it, you have two of your three basic food groups covered.

4 ripe Hass avocados (pebbly dark-skinned),
   peeled and pitted
½ cup finely chopped white onion
½ cup finely chopped tomatoes
2 jalapeño peppers, minced
4 teaspoons fresh lime juice
2 cloves garlic, minced
1 teaspoon coarse sea salt or kosher salt,
   or ½ teaspoon regular salt
¼ cup finely chopped cilantro (optional)

Coarsely mash the avocados with a fork. Stir in the onion, tomatoes, jalapeños, lime juice, garlic, and salt. Serve immediately, or cover with plastic wrap, pressing the wrap onto the surface of the guaca-mole, and refrigerate for up to 4 hours. Garnish with the cilantro, if you like, just before serving.

Margarita Salsa

A perfect fusion of spicy salsa with the fire of tequila, kissed with lots of citrus zing from Grand Marnier, fresh orange, and zesty lime.

2 cups chopped tomatoes
½ cup finely chopped white onion
½ cup minced fresh cilantro
2 tablespoons chopped peeled orange segments
2 jalapeño peppers, minced
4 cloves garlic, minced
4 teaspoons gold tequila
4 teaspoons Grand Marnier
2 teaspoons fresh lime juice
1 teaspoon salt
½ teaspoon very finely grated lime zest

In a medium bowl, combine all the ingredients. Cover and refrigerate for 1 to 2 hours to blend the flavors.

Spicy Black Bean Dip

There is nothing more delicious or satisfying than making your own fresh bean dip, and this tasty and timeless recipe is so uncomplicated you can whip one up pronto. The smooth tangle of textures is infused with spices, jazzed up with chipotle chiles, and mellowed out with Jack cheese. I guarantee, once you taste this fabulous homemade bean dip, you'll never go back to that canned stuff again.

2 cans (15 ounces each) black beans, undrained

4 slices bacon

1 cup chopped onion

1 cup chopped red bell pepper

2 cloves garlic, minced

½ to 1 teaspoon red pepper flakes
   or minced chipotle en adobo

½ teaspoon ground cumin

½ teaspoon dried oregano, crushed

1 cup chopped tomatoes

1¼ cups (5 ounces) shredded pepper Jack
   or Monterey Jack cheese

2 teaspoons fresh lime juice

Salt and freshly ground black pepper

½ cup sour cream

2 tablespoons chopped fresh cilantro

In a food processor, purée 1 can of the beans with its liquid; set aside. Drain the remaining can of beans; set aside. Cook the bacon in a large skillet over medium heat until crisp. Drain on paper towels; crumble and refrigerate. Pour off all but 1 tablespoon of bacon drippings from the skillet. Add the onion, bell pepper, and garlic to the skillet; cook until tender. Stir in the red pepper flakes, cumin, and oregano; cook, stirring, for 1 minute. Stir in both cans of beans and the tomatoes. Cook, stirring often, until the mixture thickens slightly, 3 to 4 minutes. Remove from heat. Stir in the cheese and lime juice; season with salt and pepper. Cover and refrigerate for at least several hours or overnight, until thickened. Stir in half of the bacon. Top with sour cream, cilantro, and the remaining bacon.

Southwest Layered Bean Dip

Spread Spicy Black Bean Dip (above) in the bottom of an 8-cup serving dish. Spread Killer Guacamole (page 100) on top. Spread 1 cup sour cream on top. Garnish with chopped tomatoes, chopped fresh cilantro, chopped olives, and shredded Monterey Jack or Cheddar cheese. Makes about 8 cups.

Chile con Queso

This ultra-cheesy, spicy dip is nothing short of heaven—the food of the gods! It's a classic combination of Jack and Velveeta cheese (yes, Velveeta—trust me on this one) and fresh ripe tomatoes, all fired up with chiles. The onions, chiles, and garlic are even better when roasted. And if you're pinched for time, you can substitute some pico de gallo in place of the onions, tomatoes, and garlic. Keep it warm in a Crockpot, and serve it up with a big bowl of tortilla chips with more on hand, 'cause this dip will go fast!

24 Anaheim chiles (about 4 pounds)
1 pound Velveeta cheese, cubed
3 cups shredded Monterey Jack cheese
1 cup heavy cream
4 cups finely chopped white onion
2 cups chopped tomatoes
4 cloves garlic, minced

Preheat the broiler. Cut the chiles in half lengthwise; remove the stems. Place, cut-side down, on a foil-lined baking sheet and flatten with the palm of your hand. Broil 3 inches from the heat until charred. Transfer to a paper bag, seal, and let steam for 10 minutes to soften skins. Remove and discard the skins; chop the chiles (you should have about 3 cups chopped chile). Set aside.

In a 4-quart saucepan (or use a double boiler), melt the cheeses over low heat, stirring constantly. Stir in the cream, and cook, stirring, until almost smooth. Stir in the chiles, onion, tomatoes, and garlic. Heat through. Serve in a chafing dish or fondue pot.

hot tip

For over-the-top queso, roast the onion and garlic. And for extra flavor, add chopped chipotles en adobo.

Smokin' Chipotle Dip

There's nothing better than a great party dip, and this one's got it all!
Picante peppers and fresh cilantro are fired up with the smoky heat of
chipotle chiles, cooled down with sour cream, and fueled with a
splash of tequila to give this ultra-creamy dip that extra bite. So dive
on in with tortilla chips, or even better, dipping vegetables.

2 cups sour cream

1 cup mayonnaise

1½ cups finely chopped white onion

⅔ cup finely chopped yellow bell pepper

½ cup minced fresh cilantro

6 tablespoons minced chipotles en adobo

2 tablespoons gold tequila

6 cloves garlic, minced

½ teaspoon very finely grated lime zest

In a bowl, stir the sour cream and mayonnaise together until smooth.
Stir in the onion, bell pepper, cilantro, chipotles, tequila, garlic, and
zest. Cover and refrigerate for 1 to 2 hours to blend the flavors.

hot tip

For the weight-conscious, low-fat or fat-free sour
cream and mayonnaise can be substituted, with
fabulous results!

Miracle Margarita Flan Cake

Whoever invented this cake is a genius. It has been in my family's repertoire of favorite desserts for as long as I can remember. A culinary freak, this crazy miracle cake implodes in the pan, yet still comes out luscious! Made with all the classic ingredients of the perfect suburban 1950s dessert, it's perfumed with coconut and the zest of citrus, then laced with the orange essence of Grand Marnier and a tequila kick. I'm telling you, this cake is extremely, deliciously addictive. So throw one of these decadent desserts together for your next dinner party and impress the hell out of your guests, without having to flambé anything.

1 can (14 ounces) sweetened condensed milk

1 can (12 ounces) evaporated milk

3 eggs

3 tablespoons Grand Marnier

1 teaspoon very finely grated orange zest

Vegetable-oil cooking spray

½ cup cajeta (Mexican caramel sauce)
   or caramel ice cream topping

1 box (18.25 ounces) Butter Recipe cake mix

½ cup gold tequila

1 teaspoon very finely grated lime zest

1 cup sweetened flaked coconut

Preheat the oven to 325°F. In a large bowl, whisk the sweetened condensed milk, evaporated milk, eggs, Grand Marnier, and orange zest together. Set aside.

Generously spray a 12-cup Bundt pan with vegetable-oil spray. Spread the cajeta or caramel sauce in the bottom of the pan. Set aside.

Prepare the cake mix according to the package directions, substituting the ½ cup tequila for ½ cup of the required water, and adding lime zest. Fold coconut into the cake batter. Pour the batter on top of the cajeta in the pan. Gradually pour the milk mixture over the batter (the milk mixture will sink and the batter will rise).

Bake for 45 to 50 minutes, or until a toothpick inserted in the center comes out clean. Let cool in the pan on a wire rack for 15 minutes. Unmold onto a serving plate. Let cool completely.

Fajitas Borrachas

I have been making fajitas for thirty years, nurturing them to a level of perfection, and I think I'm finally there. This is the culmination of all my taste-testing for the ultimate fajita recipe! Now the key to great fajitas is the marinade and, not being one to limit great tequila flavor just to a glass, I've added a fiery hit of the agave juice to fresh pico de gallo, for a marinade that's hugely delicious. This recipe is so simple and easy, it's absolutely foolproof. Just marinate the steak and chicken and throw them on the grill. And if you need more heat, add some puréed chipotle chiles.

Marinade:

2 cartons (8 ounces each) fresh
    store-bought pico de gallo

¼ cup silver tequila

¼ cup fresh lime juice

¼ cup extra-virgin olive oil

6 cloves garlic, minced

1 teaspoon salt

2½ pounds skirt steak

2 pounds boneless, skinless chicken breasts,
    trimmed of fat and connective tissue

Thirty 8-inch flour tortillas

To make the marinade: In a food processor, purée all the marinade ingredients, in batches if necessary. Divide the marinade between 2 large, shallow casserole dishes. Put the steak in one dish, cover; put the chicken in the other dish, cover. Let stand at room temperature for 1 hour, turning the steak and chicken after 30 minutes.

Grill or broil the steak, about 4 minutes on each side, turning once, until medium-rare. Grill or broil the chicken, about 2 minutes on each side, turning once, until cooked through. Transfer the steak and chicken to a carving platter; cover with aluminum foil and let rest for 10 minutes.

Meanwhile, heat the tortillas, wrapped in foil, in a 350ºF oven, turning once, for 10 minutes. Slice the steak and chicken across the grain into ¼-inch strips. Serve immediately with hot tortillas and, if you like, Killer Guacamole (page 100), Margarita Salsa (page 100), and Roasted Three-Pepper Salsa (page 99).

hot tip

Substitute purchased rotisserie chickens, shredded and gently reheated, for super-quick fixin's!

Index